Shabbat

HOW TO USE THIS BOOK

Read the captions in the eight-page booklet and, using the labels beside each sticker, choose the image that best fits in the space available.

Don't forget that your stickers can be stuck down and peeled off again. If you are careful, you can use your Shabbat stickers more than once.

You can also use your Shabbat stickers to decorate your own books, or for project work at school.

First American Edition, 2005

03 04 05 10 9 8 7 6 5 4 3 2 1

Published in the United States by
DK Publishing, Inc.
375 Hudson Street
New York, New York 10014

Consultant Lenny Hort
Written by Andrea Pinnington
Designed by Chris Scollen

ISBN 0-7566-0982-8

Color reproduction by Colourscan
Printed and bound in China by L Rex.

The publisher would like to thank the following for their kind permission to reproduce their photographs:
a=above; b=below; c=centre; l=left; r=right; t=top;
DK Images: Brian Cosgrove 2tcr; Chris Mattison 4tcr; Courtesy of the British School of Falconry/Kim Taylor 3cr; Dave King 4tr; Dave King/Jeremy Hunt (modelmaker) 3crbb; Finley Holiday Film 3tcr; Francesca York 2bl, 2clb; Frank Greenaway 2br, 3bcl; Geoff Dann 4ca (leaves); Jerry Young 3cb, 3clb, 3bl, 3br, 4cra; Jewish Museum, London/Andy Crawford 7c; Julian Baum 3tcl; Kim Taylor 3c, 3crb; Max Alexander 7tl; Tim Ridley 2bc. Getty Images: Ron Dahlquist 3tl; William Smithey Jr 2tr. Impact Photos: Stewart Weirl 7crb. All other images © Dorling Kindersley www.dkimages.com
See our complete product line at
www.dk.com

LONDON, NEW YORK,
MELBOURNE, MUNICH, AND DELHI

The story of Shabbat

The Torah teaches that God created the world in six days. On the seventh day, God rested. This was the first Shabbat or Sabbath day.

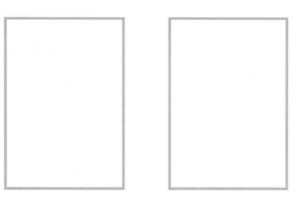

Darkness   Light   Heaven   Earth

1 **The first day**
On the first day, God made the darkness and the light.

2 **The second day**
On the second day, God made both the heaven and the earth.

3 **The third day**
On the third day, God created the land and the sea.

Land

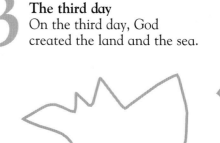

Fern

Rose

The land was brown and bare, so God covered it with all kinds of plants and trees.

Sea

Iris

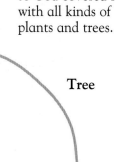

Tree

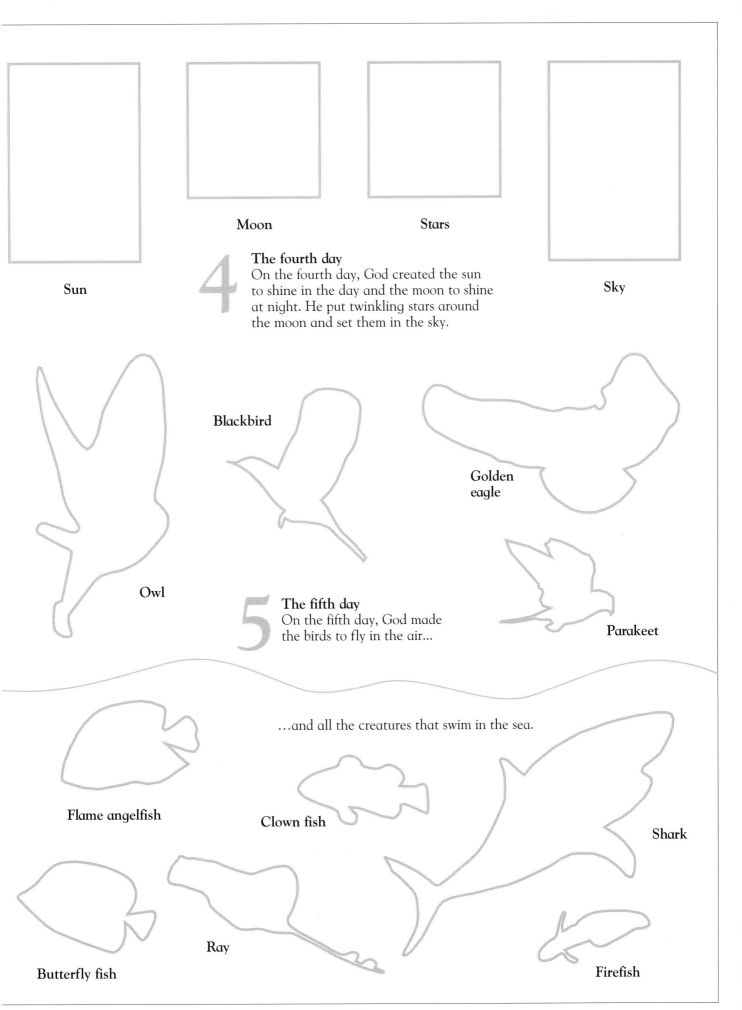

Sun

Moon

Stars

Sky

The fourth day
On the fourth day, God created the sun to shine in the day and the moon to shine at night. He put twinkling stars around the moon and set them in the sky.

Blackbird

Golden eagle

Owl

The fifth day
On the fifth day, God made the birds to fly in the air...

Parakeet

...and all the creatures that swim in the sea.

Flame angelfish

Clown fish

Shark

Butterfly fish

Ray

Firefish

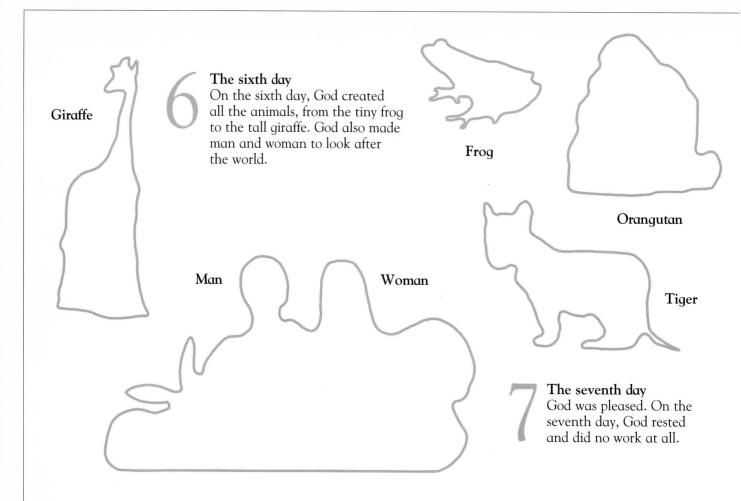

Giraffe

6 **The sixth day**
On the sixth day, God created all the animals, from the tiny frog to the tall giraffe. God also made man and woman to look after the world.

Frog

Orangutan

Man   **Woman**

Tiger

7 **The seventh day**
God was pleased. On the seventh day, God rested and did no work at all.

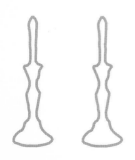

Candlesticks
The lighting of candles is important at the start of Shabbat.

How Shabbat is celebrated

Jewish families remember God's day of rest every week. This day is known as Shabbat. It begins when the sun sets on Friday and continues until Saturday at nightfall. Shabbat is a very important part of Jewish family life. These are some of the objects that are used in the home during Shabbat.

Spice box and kiddush cup
The family passes these around at different times during Shabbat.

Challah and cover
This traditional bread is eaten every Shabbat. The bread is covered with this cloth until it is time to break the bread and share it out.

Challah

Cover

Darkness

Havdalah candle

Spices

Washing hands

Clown fish

Blackbird

Firefish

Playing games

Brushing hair

Tree

Sea

Torah

Kiddush cup

The end of havdalah

Land

Heaven

Braiding

Candlestick

Moon

Candlestick

Brushing

Light

Fern

Reading

Iris

Cleaning

Ray

Special prayers

Tiger

Man and woman

Making food

Wine

Challah cover

Giraffe

Baking

Sky

Kneading

Blessing

Orangutan

Getting dressed

Prayers

Golden eagle

Challah

Eating together

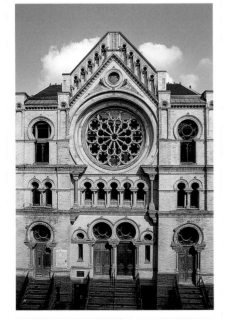

Flame angelfish

Synagogue

Sun

Butterfly fish

Stars

Sharing the challah

Lighting the candles

Earth

Holding the candle

Rose

Shark

Owl

Mixing

Parakeet

Rolling

Spice
box

Putting out the candle

The end of Shabbat

Frog

Preparing for Shabbat

All the work to make Shabbat special must be done before Shabbat starts. The house is cleaned and all the meals are prepared. Usually, every member of the family has a job to do. Here are some of the things that need to be done before Shabbat begins.

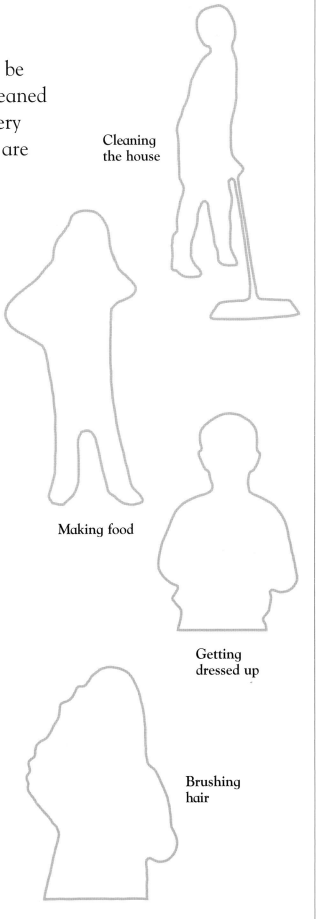

Cleaning the house

Making food

Getting dressed up

Brushing hair

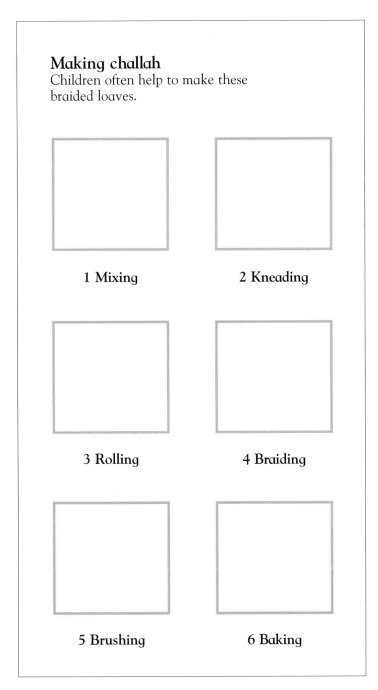

Making challah
Children often help to make these braided loaves.

1 Mixing

2 Kneading

3 Rolling

4 Braiding

5 Brushing

6 Baking

5

Friday nights

The home is the center of Shabbat celebrations. Most Jewish families have a special meal together on Friday nights. It is a time to enjoy the gifts given by God. During Shabbat, Jews wish each other *Shabbat shalom*, which means "Sabbath peace."

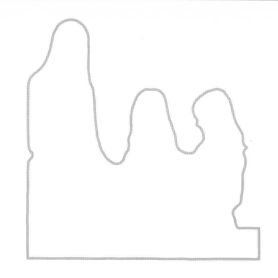

Lighting the candles
We light and bless candles before sunset on Fridays to mark the start of Shabbat.

Blessing the children
After the Shabbat candles are lit, the parents bless their children.

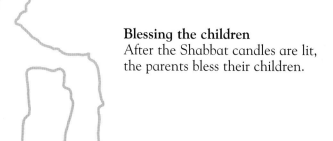

Blessing the wine and challah
Special prayers thanking God for the food and drink are said over the wine or juice and challah.

Before the meal

Washing hands
Two cups of water are poured on each hand using a washing cup and bowl.

Sharing the challah
Then the challah is uncovered, sprinkled with salt, and shared.

Eating together
After the blessings, we eat dinner and talk about the week.

Saturdays

On Saturday mornings, many families go to synagogues for morning prayers. They then go home for a meal, often inviting guests to go with them. After lunch, everyone rests and relaxes. This may mean a trip to the park to play with friends, or it may mean a quiet time at home.

Going to synagogue
A synagogue or temple is where Jewish people meet to pray and worship.

The Torah
Every Shabbat, a new portion of the torah is read and discussed in synagogues.

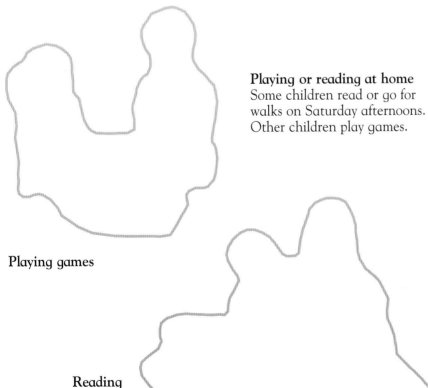

Playing games

Reading

Playing or reading at home
Some children read or go for walks on Saturday afternoons. Other children play games.

Prayer time
Many prayers are said during Shabbat. Every prayer has a special meaning and helps us remember the importance of the Sabbath day.

Havdalah

At the end of Shabbat, it is time for havdalah. This is when families say good-bye to the day of rest and look forward to working again. At this time, a short service takes place that helps to carry forward the sweetness and holiness of the Sabbath day into the week ahead.

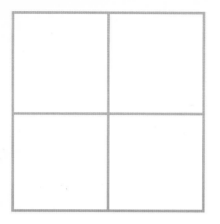

The end of the Shabbat
Shabbat is said to be over when three stars appear in the sky on Saturday evening.

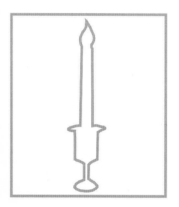

The start of the ceremony
The lights are turned off and the many wicks of the braided havdalah candle are lit.

Smelling the spices
A spice box is passed round and everyone breathes in the sweet smell to remember it for the coming week.

Looking at the candle
The havdalah candle is held up high and everyone puts a hand up to the light.

Sipping the wine
The wine or grape juice is blessed and the cup is passed around the family.

Putting out the candle
The candle flame is put out in the wine.

The end of havdalah
Finally, the family wishes one another a healthy happy week with the words *Shavua tov*.